An

ACCIDENTAL

Diary

An
ACCIDENTAL
Diary

A sonnet a week for a year

by Robert R. Bowie, Jr.

Revised Edition, 2025
ISBN 978-1-62806-445-2 (hardcover)
ISBN 978-1-62806-444-5 (softcover)
ISBN 978-1-62806-446-9 (ebook)
LCCN 2025905025

Published by Salt Water Media
29 Broad Street, Suite 104
Berlin, MD 21811
www.saltwatermedia.com
Printed in the USA.

Designed by B. Creative Group, Inc.
Art direction by Kerry Skarda

Photography by Robert R. Bowie, Jr.

Author website: www.RobertBowieJr.com

To Susan and our families,
past and present,
and to our friends
who carry us with them.

———

To my mentors,
Elisabeth Bishop,
Professor William Alfred
and Candace Currie.

Introduction

Almost twenty years ago, I became determined to learn
how to write a sonnet. Because I didn't know another way,
I decided to write a sonnet a week for a year. To meet
my deadline, I asked a friend if we could exchange our
drafts each Monday morning by 8:30 for fifty-two
consecutive weeks.

Since I was focused on the technical requirements of a
sonnet I didn't really concern myself with the subject matter.
Every sonnet turned out to be a random thought I had
during the week or some idea, coming late Sunday night as
I struggled to meet my deadline. After that year I pretty
much forgot about them.

Over the last few years, as I have dedicated my life to
writing, I rediscovered them. What caught my eye first was
how uninhibited they were. Because none of this was
intended to see the light of day there had been no
self-censorship. I had written about an afternoon blizzard
in Baltimore, skateboarders in the park, skinny-dipping
advice for my children, predestination and Boston's
debutante parties, driving through Baltimore's harbor
tunnel with the top down, my fear of dying alone, the
wonderfulness of ex-girlfriends who have forgiven you,
being tricked into scuba diving with sharks, family lobster
dinners, lust, love, memory, imagination, even giving
up smoking.

Although they met the technical requirements of a sonnet they were different than traditional sonnets. They were little stories or pictures which now, read chronologically as weekly chapters, revealed themes. I could see how each week I developed more confidence and craftmanship. As the year progressed, music and nice rhythms came into the lines, even a senseof humor appeared, and a wide range of feelings were unexpectedly on display.

This book turned out to be an exercise in accidental spontaneity. If I occasionally make you laugh, I have succeeded.

Robert R. Bowie, Jr.
2021

City Snow

(Bolton Hill)

From a four o'clock sky the first snowflakes fall
To settle down on trafficked city streets.
Each snowflake falls separately, till all
Conspire to hide the city like a secret.

The last street lights go on, and the snow reflects
Upon the domiciliary landscape.
The more snow falls the less you really expect
The city to be what it's supposed to be:

It becomes a beautiful blinking shape,
An image of slowing inactivity,
Slowing into snow drifts. It snows very late.
A pronouncement of peace subdues the city.

The drifting snow controls the city violence
With a voice made entirely of silence.

The Order in Things

The last swallow flies low over the lake.
The thick fir trees become the first darkness
Gathering along the shore. Leaves cease to shake.
The dusk foreshadows the lake's silence.

The deep quiet is its own diversion.
The world is peaceful. My thoughts my own.
I change places but not location
As the mind takes in the scene and is alone.

Standing cold here on the dock tonight
I think about the fish roaming hungry
Below while the preying birds in their flight
Circle above. Held in tranquility

Is the bird above and the fish below,
As order in moments that come and go.

Six Days Without Cigarettes

A big broad smile opens across his face
And his eyes are wide with new confidence.
He's a six-year-old boy who has found his place.
Sleep has released a house that was once tense

And now he sits with his father, together
Up late, a victor in the game of hearts.
We exit into the summer weather.
We both have agreed to play a thousand parts,

Man and boy, each in the welcome dark.
Up on my shoulders as we walk the dog
The reservoir calls like an amusement park
With its thick vines, deep water and rotting logs.

Trouble? I'm six days without cigarettes.
It's all for him —I'd kill without regrets.

Dred Scott's Revenge

Perfectly placed in the restricted space
Roger Brooke Taney, now deep green in bronze,
Divides the traffic in Mount Vernon Place.
Around him each night the streetlights go on

And cast him in ageless, shifting shadows,
While he's stared down by headlights that turn and go
Past his park. Not so very long ago
He was the master of his age. But shows

Of daily disrespect: urinating dogs,
The bums drinking from bagged bottles below him,
The unconscious passing traffic and fogs
That come from the harbor to roll on in

Around him, confirm the indication
That the past is just an aberration.

Belief

(Mayan city of Tikal, November 29, 1995)

The stars over Tikal are frightening and bright.
I am here, on sacred land, in the jungle
Before dawn in the Guatemalan night.
The moisture and pre-morning has its smell

But I modernize the scent with the smoke
From a little match to light my cigarette.
Cesar comes through the door drinking a Coke.
He says he knew the others would all forget.

He won't take me into the ruins alone.
Down the dark path, I follow my flashlight
Into the past, to where time has made its home,
Into the temple and sacrificial sites

Where people of belief played their cosmic part
And reached through ribs to hold high a human heart.

Late-Life Lust

Late in life lust comes so indiscreetly
After the blind routine kills everything
In its smooth odometer-clicking way.
The time becomes years of weather changing;

The pendulum of steady windshield wipers
On the long way there and the long way back.
I lost my wife to kids and dirty diapers.
Most men do. I smile. She doesn't smile back.

Anyway, in the prison of my days
A phone call came. An old girlfriend's voice singing.
Her song was full of our old reckless ways
And my mind filled with bed headboard-banging.

I love my wife and I will do what I must
But still I linger with this late-life lust.

Sunday Night Dinner
(The Vegan Argument)

Off with the lid of the fast-boiling pot.
With white wine in a glass in my left hand
And with its tail clenched in its repeating knot
And feeling the steam, which it understands,

Is a lobster, tonight's dinner, in my right.
But all along its thrashing tail and legs
Thick, fresh and glassy in the kitchen's light
Are thousands upon thousands of her eggs

Expelled as her last act of preservation.
Now above the boiling water she lies,
Claws forced shut, on her back, in my occasion.
Far from home her children cannot survive.

Hungry, interested as an observer,
Like a god. Beyond hope or help, I hold her.

Domestic Discord & My Fear of Dying Alone

Late, now in the last few days of my death
I pack my desk and drive through falling leaves
And cannot sleep and cannot catch my breath.
No oxygen in a world of leafless trees.

My children are safe at a neighbor's home.
The hospice workers come in and unpack.
They tell me when I die I'll not be alone
But they won't leave until I can't come back.

All those things I will never see again
In this life of long days and short years.
Now distant lightening hits and I feel pain.
Is it rain? Is it thunder? Is it tears?

Is suffering unique? Is the fist uncurled
With my last breath as I inhale the world?

Vacant Buildings

Tonight these vacant buildings torture me.
My flaws are like random burning light bulbs,
Left burning by construction men. With the
Last lock latched in every door a great bulge

Of light increases with the coming night.
The workmen all just don't care and leave their
Error to be recognized. It's black and white.
It's wrong and right. Darkness is everywhere.

I am darkness when darkness is disturbed.
Talk it out? This is how I know my flaws:
Silent buildings with lights left on for words
As my hollow head holds darkness in its jaws.

Forgive me what I do not say to you
As I window my inexactitude.

My Old Landlady
(or Why I Fear the 21st Century – Part 1)

The lowdown my landlady has on me
Would bring a lowlife alive, and it does.
My endless paper reading stacks up. She
Sifts through my trash to find out what I was

Last week. She has a passkey to my mind
And does not hesitate to use it when
Her geriatric legs will pain to find
Three flights up, in my room, a better life than

She can understand in just one visit;
So she comes again, creaking up the stairs,
Turns the key, finds a letter, and wonders if
It will put the puzzle into place. Where

I live, I lease from her; but I will be
Always different than what she thinks of me.

Life Is a Bic

Within the four corners of the blank page
Lives the life's work of a ballpoint pen
And the untranslatable language
Of its beginnings and of its end.

It plays at drawing doodle-faces,
Or stringing words to make a thought brought pure,
Or works the architecture of spaces,
Or the ego of a grand signature.

It seems to enjoy this, its universe.
Even if it's dotted i's or crossed t's
And all work and no play has been its curse.
It can record the life we live and breathe

But how entirely unlike your life or mine
Is a single thin line as a life defined?

High School Crew

In the early spring, when I turned fifteen,
My choices were baseball, tennis or crew.
Between Boston and Cambridge I had seen
Rhythmic oars of singles, eights, fours and twos

Beneath the bridges of the Charles River.
I was appointed stroke. I paced the boat.
Like a surgeon's stitch our sharp blades suture
The shell's trailing razor cut as each stroke

Drives us through the smooth and glassy water
And leaves no scar. The coxswain pounds out,
On the gunnels, the rhythm of my order.
Tin cans and prophylactics float past the boat.

Our smooth and perfect rhythmic mantra broke
Beneath the bridges, into echoes: "Stroke. Stroke."

Death Penalty Defendant Waiting for His Verdict

(Baltimore Courtroom)

You be in this box of artificial light.
It feels like a hothouse where nothing blooms
Under this neon ceiling that burns all night.
Where is the daylight in this damn courtroom?

Why doesn't the jury already know?
My lawyer says, "Let them deliberate."
And then goes out with the D.A. for a smoke.
I heard them laugh about "it getting late."

Tell me, what is a crime against the State?
The guy bitch-slapped my girlfriend and took her hat.
Trust me, he had this death wish that couldn't wait
But my lawyer never told it just like that.

God, I want to leave this room and be free.
The jury enters but doesn't look at me.

Belief on Escher's Chessboard

Am I atoms and DNA that begets,
The consciousness in collected cells,
(Unconscious of what they will not forget)
Of being born in cold tidal wishing wells?

At the edges of this world and my heart,
Past the farthest boundary of my reach and grasp
Where ideas cause worlds to fall apart
Is where we live and love and cannot last.

Dust is it, but is not really it at all?
Do cells dance like dice in a gamblers hell?
Is God just outside the sound of "his" own call
And all of this some accidental spell?

We guess, speculate, conclude and grow old.
So Belief answers what we cannot know?

The Facts of Life

I swam, back then, with some fathers' daughters,
Backstroking only slightly out of touch,
Out to the raft in the starry waters
And never thought of their fathers all that much.

My child, don't judge me till you're fifty-five
But there were midnight visits to Ice House Pond,
In my misspent youth, when I was still alive,
Where couples would strip, and swim and then bond.

And my child, this I know for sure is true:
At seventeen we all are born to be free
But 'cause I'm your father and I love you
Please consider this seasoned advice from me:

As you lust for life avoid the crudity
But don't miss occasional sponti-nudity.

My Little Stone Buddha

As a glass eye looks into the abyss,
The little stone Buddha, on the bookshelf top,
Sits as a symbol of inner peace and bliss;
But as symbol is he what he is not?

Is he not just my sculpted end of pain?
The mirror looks back into my old eyes,
And my old eyes look back at me insane.
Tonight, the pain is deep. Can't that glass eye cry?

Is everything only symbolic meaning?
Sure, why not? Probably even for him:
Crosses, numbers, alphabets for reading;
Is he not made from me and my dark within?

Does not the self, not the Buddha, hold the bliss?
We make much of nothing, which is all of this.

Growing Gracefully Old

With this cold and the first of this new year
I have felt so out of season but of late
I have felt soft roots go down. I felt fear
Of change that I did not anticipate.

Before I didn't know I was a seed
Safe, buried alive and so self-contained.
Before, I defined myself by my need.
Before, I was perfect and self-explained.

How is it I've become my own belief?
How odd that my thoughts have new gravity?
I'm relieved without searching for relief.
My pupils dilate to amity.

Reborn in the dark September of the man;
How odd that I have become who I am.

Sleeping on the Porch

I sit in a screened-in porch in Oxford,
Maryland as the hot summer evening comes
With western colors that fall on docks for
Commerce and docks for lucky rich-born sons

Who laugh as they lower luffing sailboat sails.
A storm is gathering over the bay.
To the west long languid nimbus clouds trail
In the sunset like soldiers who walked away

And rested in the fields not knowing war
Was just about to come. A cool wind picks up.
Two girls leave and once inside, shut the door.
Quiet. The thunderhead's attack is abrupt.

It laces the sky with long deep bright lightning.
I wake to see eastern water brightening.

Buddy Reports
(Why I Fear the 21st Century – Part 2)

With the third of three quick and violent punches
I laid him out in the fresh long green grass.
The laughing crowd left in laughing bunches.
I pulled the crying boy up off his ass.

In the first two weeks of our ninth-grade year
We were exposed to wilderness and "Buddy
Reports." Buddy Reports were to be feared.
For two weeks it rained cold and was muddy.

We suffered at our chores and in our tents.
One boy trapped a raccoon and took it to where
He drowned it in the lake. The lake's suspense
Broke as its hand reached up and gripped the air.

Buddy Reports shaped our society.
We told on each other so easily.

Heaven

I find a seat without making a sound.
In the dark the old air conditioner
Cools this amateur theater in the round.
I wait and become the listener.

I've had three plays performed here years ago.
I know the sound even before the lights
Come up and the actors begin the show.
They act their lives out on weekend nights.

They give up what they have, forsaking plans
To find real-life loved ones or a cause...
The hand holding breaks into clapping hands
And though it cannot gather to applause,

It still resounds, echoes and repeats
In this little theater of empty seats.

My Airport Lounge Conversion

"Your Loran or Celestial Navigation
Tracks only satellites or stars and provides
Nothing more than physical location..."
Is this airport prophet changing people's lives?

Two guys turn away from the bar TV
And stop popping peanuts to glance his way.
He's born again and ready to set me free.
When I turn, he tells me to have a nice day.

In the bathroom I relax into a whiz.
I smile at the thought as I flush and leave.
We're really not that different. It is
Easy to become overwhelmed by the

Present day and it is such a relief
That much of life comes down to just belief.

Smoke & Mirrors

(San Jose, Belize)

The cherub-cheeked patrons of the local bar
Have watched me light my cigarette and breathe
Deep — another "smoke break" — I glance out far...
Then back to my story... but did they all leave?

That's how I imagine it now in dreams,
Which wake me from nightmare-restless sleep.
The cigarettes will kill me it now seems,
And the disappearing company I keep.

No excuse will ever do. I must quit.
Now in the second day of self-hate, again
I drink scotch and continue "to commit"
To save myself. Why do I endure this pain?

The claws are in my lungs and my head aches
As I drink and pray that it's not too late.

No Boundaries of Dusk or Dawn

Ah yes, I have this other place I live
Past the courtrooms and domestic disputes.
I am "on" when I get "off" as I give
Those goodbye, dead-eyed, after-work salutes.

My world comes alive late at night with scotch
And jazz CDs and books that others write.
A mind's life can thrive in an empty box
When I light fires and stay up too late at night.

Shakespeare got me through law school, that I know.
He told me sweet stories on weekend nights.
Here, friends, from off the shelf, they come and go.
Shouldn't this all die when I turn "off" the lights?

Why do I live in, and off of, when I'm "on"?
There really are no boundaries of dusk or dawn.

Sunday Accidentally Spent

I'm by the pool on this sunny Sunday
With my wife and two children off at church.
I've pulled the Bible off the shelf, on display,
From its front-row center prominent perch.

I'll read it after the New York Times.
Midway through The Book Review I half-see
A Monarch butterfly in the sunshine,
Hold the book like a Christian wannabe.

Once you hold the Times it's history.
Finished. Forgotten. Trash-canned people's dreams
But the Bible and butterfly as extremes?
The ancient code and the fatally free?

Did the two of them touch by accident
And was my Sunday accidentally spent?

The Buddha of the Beach

(Little Cayman, March '03)

See, it all happened in the aqua bleach
Of light, when, bright past all expectations
I became the sunburned Buddha of this beach.
Nirvana? Sure, I answered all my questions.

Will everything around me be eaten
Whether in the air or in the ocean?
Why yes, nothing wins here or is beaten.
Is Impermanence all re-creation...?

The dive boats round the cut each day at dawn.
I lose the time in my usual ways.
The sun is like a light bulb that's always on
And in time I start to lose track of days

And come to see how things all die and breed
And the excellence between these extremes.

The Parking Garage

What if "form follows function" went too far?
Say, like take my parking garage. It seems
To inhale all of these exhausted cars
And then stacks them on levels A to Z.

How Bauhaus, is endless suburban sprawl?
The elevators speak mechanically:
"Elevator up." "Elevator down." All
So blind drivers feel no inadequacy?

This form is not born from a "designer's fire."
My key on level Z, which I can't find,
Made the locks, like the roads make the tire.
Is this form born from the function of the mind?

Yes, and like a lover's arms, this edi-fice,
Cradles my engine in its man-made space.

The Present Creation
(The Gospel According to a Boston Cab Driver)

The tulip poplars bloom block by block down
Beacon Street on this perfect day in May
And as we catch the lights and blow through town
The cabby turns his head around to say:

"On days like this, tell me there ain't no God."
The day and his tone demand you get caught
Up in his thought and listen. "Its real odd
How those Darwin guys so completely bought

"Into if the Bible got the timing wrong
There can't be no creator. Just look at this!
Who cares if from some monkeys we were born?
Trust me pal, nothing here is hit or miss.

"It's like they believe in chickens, but their heads
Get turned around so they don't believe in eggs."

I Could Justify Anything

(Boston Debutant Parties of the Early '70s)

In a tuxedo at a circular
Table sitting with a woman in blue
Who explained life as a spectacular
"Boom" that sent atoms out "so I could meet you"

Brings me back to that clock universe thing
Where the Center is made and is making
Everything, and preordained has always been
The steps of the next dance … so I'm thinking

I'm guilt-free in a predestined universe?
The music picks up and she is so hot.
Her hips are moving and what is much worse,
I am thinking to myself "why," then "why not"?

For who cares if I remember and regret
I'm dancing these steps as a marionette.

Predawn Swim

The fireflies burn out well beneath the stars
And leave the shadows of the trees around me,
Naked here, in a galaxy at war.
Poolside, in my moon reflection, I will be

Dropping out of this humid world down to
The unexpected. Guillotined to cold;
Feet first with the water closing over you
And then shoving off the pool bottom, old

And stretching out as the new world runs by
Drifting utterly empty, my life gone
In my underwater wake and my eyes
Closed till I hit the wall and stand alone

In the shallow end, and I am reborn,
Baptized. I rise, with the coming of the morn.

Circe Laughing at Her Swine

Circe mans the cash register and smiles
And says: "Everything here is now on sale."
Inch by inch the local mall spreads for miles
Across the country on a grander scale.

"I own them when they spend more than they've got
For nothing will satisfy their hunger
For what the TV tells them they are not.
Look, they'll buy anything to seem younger

"But soon they hate the face in the mirror.
Your Puritan ancestors take it hard
After they came for God and nothing more."
She laughs as she takes my credit card.

"You fools forgot as you turn to beasts
That enough is just as good as a feast."

Circe Laughing
at Her Swine

The Fool's Logic & Making Up Your Mind

With the top down, speeding toward the Harbor
Tunnel in the Baltimore midday heat,
Blasting Philip Glass and his sound and more
Overload than the brain can make complete,

My unresolved mind has made itself up
Concluding in patterns all of its own...
Then uncertainty comes to interrupt
The logic of that highway heading home.

I slow to pay the tunnel toll and speed
Up into the tiled darkness and its sound.
Is all my logic governed by my need?
What you think you want sure turns my head around.

The tunnel kills the scream. It's true. Once you
Make your mind up, won't any reason do?

I Love My Family

While waiting for a single-engine plane
By a grass runway at the edge of hell
I feel the evening come and watch the rain
And when the last flight is at last cancelled

I feel the breeze come from some broken window.
It gathers and it recreates its self
Perhaps from its beginnings, I don't know,
From that primal place which remakes its self.

How much I love you is what you must know.
It gathers and it recreates its self
At the center of my own cold zero
From that primal place which remakes itself.

Comfort comes only from my loved ones' sounds
When eye meets eye to pass a smile around.

The Party in My Head

I woke up this morning in the darkness
And I woke with the need for morning light.
All night my mind made people that I guess
Were made up for the dreams I had last night.

It's like my brain is like some bag lady,
Controlling, self-examining, so smart;
Gathering bits and pieces on her way:
The Greek Oracle with a shopping cart.

But what if she flunks her own quick quizzes,
And dreams some life that isn't, and never was,
And I'm caught between my life as it is
And her dreaming and what her dreaming does.

I'm just glad her friends head home with the sun
Because they've been having way too much fun!

Iris Versicolor

Here, self-preservation is metaphor:
Two dry riverbeds that run the water
From my neighborhood to the reservoir
Hold the water when it rains, in order

That a semi-septic self-made swamp pond
On two grandfathered acres, that won't perk,
Might be the birthplace of this flower on
This shallow marsh. Each spring I watch her birth.

The blue flag out of the iris family,
Has a throat of spectacled gold, and grows tall
On a solid single stem; fun, friendly
But at her roots she's poisonous to all.

Self-preservation, as final duty,
Creates its own narcissistic beauty.

Summer Thunderstorms

As with the generations long since dead
The fire and brimstone of the status quo
Wakes him up from the safety of his bed
And lightening frames him in the window

And photographs him in its afterglow.
Tonight he feels his present and its past
As the summer storm also comes and goes.
Conclusions are foolish in a world so vast.

For at the edges of his world and heart
Far past the farthest boundary of his grasp
Where ideas cause worlds to come apart
He lives in this place that will not last.

He loves his life more than he can explain
And leaves the window open to hear the rain.

Two Blind Armies

This old cemetery is so lonely.
Its thoughtful atmosphere refines with time
And ages in random eternity.
Not all that long ago Lee's double-time

Drove his troops to battle some sixty miles
Ahead of him. July heat collected
On Gettysburg. Five wide, the single line
Of Union Blue, unsure, but connected,

Stretched like an artery from Baltimore.
Two blind armies collided at this town,
And shed blood on stones which now mark this war.
In three days thousands died, then dusk came down.

Here lie the strategies of rolling dice.
Imagine, if you can, you were one life.

Returning to Tikal with My Daughter

The exchanging of colored currency
As soldiers lounged and smoked their cigarettes
While an old woman washed clothes in the stream
Should have been enough to never forget,

But I wanted to show her so much more.
We crossed the bridge into Guatemala
And into the land of the living poor.
Skinny dogs and pigs with hanging tits wallow

In the roadside brush as we both bus by.
Not even Tikal, ancient in starlight,
In its totalitarian demise,
Got the primal message exactly right,

But heading home, past pack boys with a load,
A twelve-foot boa stretched across the road.

The Heron

A tall shadow controls my autumn pond.
It moves on long legs and will stare and wait.
After the late March ice had come and gone
And the exchanged songs of the frogs that mate,

The lily pads rise through the clear water
To shelter the colonies of black tadpoles
That are born as eggs, like pupiled eyes, pure,
And, like the rest here, uncompromising souls.

The summer heat reveals the baby fish
Spawned by the survivors of last winter.
By August it is like my winter wish:
Blooming like some Eden, ready to enter.

The heron knows nothing of what I mean.
By noon it will have picked the pond all clean.

The First Spring

In my mind I can recreate the breeze
That gathered me and took me into spring
While the snow melted after the last freeze
And my life as a boy was beginning.

Out the kitchen door, still eating something,
Late and half running as I pulled the books
Onto my back and headed downhill, being
For the first time the product of my looks.

How could life have become so inviting?
How could the world warm with the thoughts of girls?
How could the clock of a planet spinning
Harmonize with these two so perfect worlds?

Odd how I can create that breeze today
And that boy comes alive in yesterday.

My Father

In the end it's touch that holds memory.
The other senses are immediate
And defend the present territory.
The other four are there to navigate.

Tonight my father went under the knife
And I waited alone with my cell phone
To see what would become of this one life;
Together, separate, and both alone.

For an hour in the last waiting room,
I remembered him as sound and insight,
Too perspicacious for the cool boxed room
That would contain him in this, his last night.

At ninety-four how could he have survived?
I kissed the forehead of a man, alive.

Great Teachers

Classrooms without students are so empty.
They are much more empty than just a room.
They're a place where learning is meant to be.
Without great teaching they become vacuums.

Walls are in danger that they may cave in.
Entire campus buildings may implode
As time rolls back into what might have been:
If no steps, then no path, and so no road.

In a hall, because no classroom will be
Open for us to talk about my daughter,
Mary Shoemaker sits across from me
And recalls the Whitman that she taught her.

She's a teacher my daughter brags about.
She lit the spark that blew her windows out.

The Marathon Man

In a world of educated guesses
About ones loves, integrity and health
It is my custom to keep promises,
Even if they are only to myself;

Still being a tenth of a ton and all,
With sacred dictates of my religion
Requiring too much food and alcohol,
What made me train to run a marathon?

I trained on a treadmill, March to July.
Got my first runner's high at fifty-five.
Depleted my life's endorphin supply,
And blew out both knees and I begged to die.

Ah yes, but to hell with all of this fun;
Next year, for sure, I'll be ready to run.

Lust and Love

His object of affection (but not of mine),
A belly button, seductively displayed,
Below the shirt which hides nipple ring outlines,
That make both her breasts look like hand grenades.

He looks for the screwdriver he has lost.
His is the world of replaceable parts.
Unscrew her belly button, her ass falls off?
Still they both dress to win the other's heart.

The city's suburbs spread out around them both
As they skateboard the parking lots and clocks
Keep the time and administer the oaths.
Is there no place left to think outside the box?

Is the message of the world we are part of
That we live so long as we lust and love?

Past Girlfriends

Was it the loss of accidental love
Or real love and an accidental loss,
Both, or maybe neither of the above?
No matter, it ended, despite some cost.

Past girlfriends are friends a lucky man will have
After mathematical random greetings
In a living generation that laughs
At any thought of predestined meetings.

They have families and their children
And they love their husbands so very much
But they are kind enough to meet you when
You come into town and ask them out to lunch.

God bless them all. They've done what really counts.
They've forgiven you completely, at least once.

My Love

Reborn again with this, the first beginnings,
And so the universe began to grow.
This time the Big Bang creates everything,
Some four point six plus billion years ago.

With its blast of atoms it made me such
Good friends that, by pure accident are mine.
For truly the accident of their touch
Is what for me, transcends this waste of time.

They say, spinning out through the atmosphere
Four billion years ago, this molten mass
Fell into the orbit that brought us here.
I know nothing in this universe will last

True, but my love transcends this existence
And the consciousness of its impermanence.

The Janitor in the Classroom

I stopped to watch him clean the window glass
And wet-mop the floor and make real sure
The day's questions, unanswered, or unasked
Were washed from blackboards and the doors secured.

"His kids," he calls them, who went home today;
They live the life-changing experiment,
Which is to navigate the unknown way
To save the future which we have not spent.

An old man's mind makes orderly his past
But lives as the victim of his future.
He washes sinks and wipes the window glass
And prepares the classroom to make sure

The desks line up in geometric rows.
What they will learn will save him, this he knows.

The Poet's Job

"The poet's job is to bring a vision
To life." The words echo and bounce around
And create discord in my mind as one
Thought turns into two only to compound.

How can the same words be two different thoughts?
Is it to bring a new vision alive?
Or a vision to the living? What's caught
As discord in harmony can survive?

But how can two thoughts harmonize as one?
Perhaps like our two eyes learn to focus?
The poet's job is to bring a vision:
It's a fresh focus to live within us.

The poet's job is to bring that vision:
To harmonize discord and these two as one.

Santa

Like a massive multicolored parachute
His boxers have collapsed upon the floor
Slightly south of a wrinkled Santa suit
That was left just outside the bathroom door.

A bunch of imagined elves in repose,
Smokin' cigarettes, feet on the table,
Hangin' and laughin' 'bout Rudolf's nose
Are lovin' life as only elves are able.

Another Christmas is, at long last, past
As the fat man shampoos in the shower
And thinks of golf and summer thoughts at last.
Who's this metaphor for redemptive power?

An old fat guy driving a sled with gifts?
A father at midnight is what it is.

The Blue Hole in Belize

Was I the fool of this sinkhole of the sea
Or a pupil in this aqua ocean?
As I fly home it looks back at me
Without memory or emotion.

Three days ago, while taunting me, Miguel
Said: "You dived it but not with me before.
I dive it deep. I dive it right to hell."
He took my money but wouldn't tell me more.

Off the boat, with Miguel still behind,
We checked our gear and descended into cold,
Deeper, darker, to fear of a different kind:
Sharks. Hundreds of them. Darting from the shadows.

At the boat Miguel offered a helping hand,
Laughing. "You understand? We chummed it man."

Walking to Work from Bolton Hill

(For Ann, 1979)

How I love our spring morning walk to work.
We meet and laugh and let the bus glide by.
The future's distant harbor skyline lurks
As we fall into our familiar stride.

Our meetings are always accidental.
Pure chance, that happens so repeatedly.
Each morning it grows more predictable,
This offer of sweet rolls and black coffee,

And more expected too. Crossing at crosswalks,
Stopping at shop windows, we travel along
This same morning route together talking
Of everything. How could this love go wrong?

Our lives are drawn to a collective center.
The buildings are the highest when we enter.

Shaving My Father

(From a draft I wrote the day after my father's death at 104)

This is the last small room in which he will rest.
Every day I visit him at four o'clock.
We balloon the room with our forgiveness.
"Either this man is dead or my watch has stopped."

Two men knock on his door then wait like guests.
"Not funny for a man this close to death."
We share what only dark humor can express.
The Marx Brothers, for both of us, are the best.

The electric razor hums in my hand
As it cuts along the cheekbone and the neck.
Like a harvester on pre-winter land
I harvest thistle from earth's intellect

Across a snow bank of thin paper skin.
They zip their bag shut and leave me without him.

The Fireplace

With two cords of hardwood stacked by the door
I'm ahead of winter again this fall.
All these years with no spark, no central core.
My art? To fortify and avoid it all.

At Mount Auburn, my friend, Candace and I
Last winter, about this time, decided
To write a poem each week and agreed to try
For e-mail delivery to the other by

Monday morning, coffee time. We would do
Fifty-two: deadlines to keep us to it.
Miss Bishop and Professor Alfred too,
I hope these make you proud. Last night I lit

A new fire in an old fireplace
And dreamed I'd warmed your hands and touched your face.

About the Poet

Robert Bowie, Jr. has worked as a house painter, bartender,
lawyer, adjunct professor, poet, author, and playwright.
He lives in Maryland. His ten produced plays include *Onaje*,
which premiered with five sold-out performances at FringeNYC.
Bob's well-reviewed collection of short stories and essays,
The Older You Get, the Shorter Your Stories Should Be, is now
available at bookstores and online. **More at** *robertbowiejr.com*.